Domestic Waste and Industrial Pollutants

Editor: *Roger Vlitos*
Editorial planning: Clark Robinson Ltd
Design: David West
                   Children's Book Design
Illustrator: Ron Hayward Associates
Picture research: Cecilia Weston-Baker
Photographic Credits:
Cover and pages 4-5, 7 top and middle left, 13 bottom, 15 bottom, 18 right,
19, 21 top, 23 top and middle and 27 bottom: Topham Picture Library; page
6: Mary Evans Picture Library; pages 7 middle right and 23 bottom: Science
Photo Library; pages 7 bottom, 9 left and 12 left and right: Magnum Photos;
pages 9 right, 11 top right and 18 left: Network Photographers; pages 11
middle, 25 middle and 29: Robert Harding Library; pages 11 bottom right, 13
top, 15 top, 16 right, 21 bottom and 27 top: Environmental Picture Library;
pages 20, 22 and 26 left and right: Rex Features; page 25 top: Zul/Chapel
Studios; page 25 bottom: Eye Ubiquitous; pages 28 left and right and 29 left
inset and right inset: Roger Vlitos; page 29 top: Panos Institute.

© Aladdin Books Ltd 1990

Created and designed by
Aladdin Books Ltd
70 Old Compton Street
London W1V 5PA

First published in
Great Britain in 1990 by
Gloucester Press
96 Leonard Street
London EC2A 4RH

ISBN 0-7496-0125-6

Printed in Belgium

The publishers would like to acknowledge that the photographs reproduced
within this book have been posed by models or have been obtained from
photographic agencies.

A CIP catalogue record for this book is available from the British Library

Facts on

Domestic Waste and Industrial Pollutants

Hugh Johnstone

GLOUCESTER PRESS
London · New York · Toronto · Sydney

CONTENTS

POLLUTION IS NOT
NEW
6

SEWAGE IS SERIOUS
8

DOMESTIC WASTE
10

INDUSTRIAL
POLLUTANTS
12

WHERE DOES IT
GO ?
14

BURNING QUESTIONS
22

USEFUL RUBBISH
24

METALS
26

ORGANIC AND
PLASTIC
28

FACT FILE
30

GLOSSARY & INDEX
31   32

Just about everything we do produces waste of one form or another. The way we deal with these wastes has an immediate effect on the way we live and on our health. It also has serious consequences for the sort of world we will be living in tomorrow. Thoughtless or uncontrolled dumpings on land, in the sea, or emissions to the air, are dangerous and cause damaging pollution. They also use up the valuable energy and material resources of our planet. We can already see the damage that is being caused to our environment and need to start taking the right actions to stop things from getting worse. The facts are that most of what we call "pollutants" are the products of the way in which we choose to live today, or the result of what people have done in the past. It is clear that unless we are more careful about the way we treat our planet the human race will not have much of a future.

POLLUTION IS NOT NEW

Pollution and waste are not new problems. What is new is the scale of the problem and the ways in which it affects virtually every aspect of the way we live. Early investigations established many of the effects of coal smoke and sewage pollution but very little was done to combat them for a long time. Pollution continued to grow and was more or less accepted as one of the inevitable features of modern life in an industrial world. It took disasters like the great London smog of 1952 and the mass poisoning of Japanese villagers at Minamata by polluted foods to open our eyes to what was happening. We now realise that uncontrolled pollution will ruin the environment, can seriously threaten our lives and, at the very least, make life much less pleasant.

EARLY RECORDS

By the 1850s the Thames was so badly polluted with sewage that a cartoon showed Death rowing along it. Public outcry, and the inconvenience caused to Parliament by the stench of the "great stink of 1851", eventually led to the development of a proper sewage system.

MOUNTING PROBLEMS

The smoke from one coal fire is not much of a nuisance, but when several thousand fires are concentrated in a town conditions can become a problem. Similarly, the pollution produced by a single factory may be unpleasant but is normally manageable. When a whole industrial town is involved, however, the area is likely to suffer. Population growth means that there are a lot more of us to generate waste and create pollution. At the same time new industries have created new pollution. Most significant of these is the motor car. The emission control systems imposed in some countries have done some good, but the number of new cars worldwide means that pollution is still growing.

SEWAGE IS SERIOUS

Untreated sewage can contaminate water supplies and spread fatal diseases like cholera and typhoid. Small amounts of sewage can be discharged into rivers or lakes where nature in the form of bacteria, plants and wildlife can eat and digest it, and so break it down. But large amounts of sewage overload the natural process with organic matter and nutrients and create a pollution hazard. To prevent this, sewage is processed in a treatment works which speeds up the natural processes to give inoffensive end-products that are easier and safer to get rid of. Untreated sewage is often discharged into the sea where it is diluted and natural processes can deal with it. Long outfall pipes are used to try to keep the sewage away from the beaches but pollution still occurs.

SEWAGE PROCESSING

In the most modern sewage works raw sewage passes through screens which remove stones and other large items. Separation of solids and liquids takes place in sedimentation tanks. The liquids then pass to aeration tanks where air is bubbled through to help bacteria digest the organic material. Finally the water is passed to another sedimentation tank where the remaining sludge settles out. This leaves cleaner water to be discharged to a river or the sea. The sludge, is transferred to a digester where it is fermented. Once dried it can be used as a fertiliser if it does not contain too many heavy metals. Methane produced in the digester is used to provide power for the sewage works.

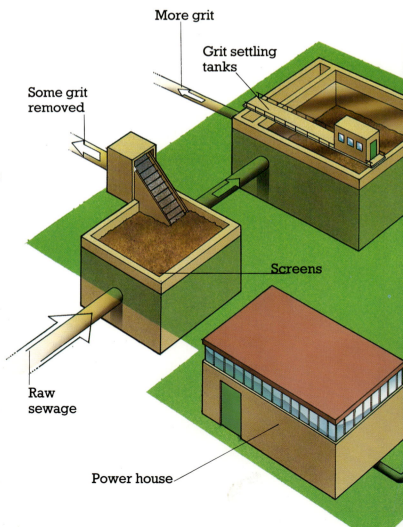

More grit

Grit settling tanks

Some grit removed

Screens

Raw sewage

Power house

USING DIRTY WATER

If there are no alternative supplies people have to use whatever water is available, even though it may be heavily polluted. If this is the case, everyday activities like washing clothes and bathing expose people to the risk of infection and poisoning.

CLEAN WATER

Clean drinking water is a basic necessity for a healthy life. But in many countries the only source of water is a polluted river or pond. Digging wells and drilling boreholes for pumps gives local people access to uncontaminated underground water.

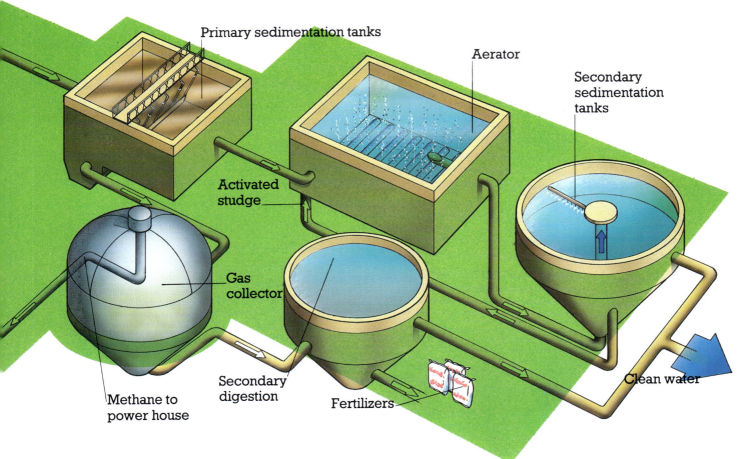

Primary sedimentation tanks

Aerator

Secondary sedimentation tanks

Activated studge

Gas collector

Methane to power house

Secondary digestion

Fertilizers

Clean water

DOMESTIC WASTE

Modern consumer society produces a lot of waste. Each of us throws away around a kilogram of rubbish each day. We have had to develop elaborate and expensive systems to get rid of refuse. Collecting waste from individual homes accounts for most of the cost but final disposal is becoming more expensive and difficult as the amount increases. The most common way of getting rid of the collected rubbish is by tipping it at landfill sites. Incineration is becoming more popular as dump sites become harder to find, but the ash still has to be dumped. This in itself can create a pollution problem if ash is allowed to blow about. Kitchen waste disposal units reduce the amount of food waste thrown in the dustbin, but they simply transfer the disposal problem to the sewage works.

THE BULK OF RUBBISH

Most of the rubbish we throw away is packaging. This includes tins, glass, plastic containers, and large amounts of paper and cardboard. In developed countries paper makes up around a third of the total rubbish with plastics, glass and metals accounting for more than a quarter. Waste food and scraps like vegetable peelings make up another quarter. Some packaging is needed to prevent products being damaged in transit, and to keep foods fresh and pure, but a lot of it is just to make the goods appear more attractive to the customer.

Original item

Card top

Remainder of pack

Outer pack

Bag

Foil case

DISPOSAL

Getting rid of bulky rubbish can be difficult and people sometimes take the easy solution of just dumping it. This creates an unsightly mess that someone else has to clear up later. To avoid this many towns have special sites where people can leave unwanted items.

CONVENIENCE FOODS

Fast food is very convenient, but the wrapping that makes it easy to take away and eat adds to the rubbish around our towns. Waste bins help keep the streets clean so long as people bother to use them but the rubbish still has to be disposed of.

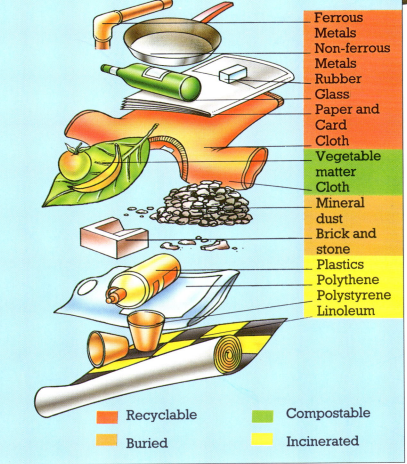

Ferrous Metals
Non-ferrous Metals
Rubber
Glass
Paper and Card
Cloth
Vegetable matter
Cloth
Mineral dust
Brick and stone
Plastics
Polythene
Polystyrene
Linoleum

Recyclable Compostable
Buried Incinerated

INDUSTRIAL POLLUTANTS

A lot of industrial waste is no more dangerous than domestic rubbish, but some of it is poisonous or inflammable. The main problem is that the sheer amount of effluent that a factory can produce is simply too much for a local environment to cope with. One common method of dealing with this type of waste is to rely on dilution. Fumes are released into the atmosphere, liquids discharged to rivers and seas, and other wastes mixed in with general rubbish. The hope was that diluting and spreading the harmful materials in this way would reduce their affects to a safe level. We are now realising that this does not work, though the effects may not be apparent for years. Accordingly, many countries have introduced strict regulations to control the types and amounts of toxic waste that can be discharged or dumped by industry.

In 1984 the world's worst industrial accident occurred in Bhopal, India. Over 2,300 died when a gas tank leaked.

BY-PRODUCTS

Waste materials that are safe in themselves can produce serious pollution if they are mishandled during disposal. Burning plastics often releases poisonous fumes and can result in the formation of highly poisonous dioxins.

POISON!

Disposal of toxic waste is often left to specialist companies. Unfortunately some of them totally fail to meet their obligations and so create an even worse hazard. Examples of this are drums of waste left standing on abandoned disposal sites, and toxic materials poured into unprotected landfills or even stockpiled in developing countries. These occurrences have given toxic waste disposal a very bad name. This makes it much more difficult for the reputable operators in the business.

Waiting for a disaster to occur! Toxic waste drums dumped instead of being dealt with.

Drums of toxic waste dumped at sea or washed overboard in a storm are washed up on the beach. More of a worry are those lost in the deep which may leak.

WHERE DOES IT GO ?

When you flush the toilet, or pull the plug out of your bath, the waste simply flows away, but where does it go? The final destination will be a river, lake or the sea. But what happens on the way? Ideally the sewage will be treated before being released into rivers or the sea. However, this is often not the case. Untreated sewage can act as a damaging fertilizer, causing excessive growth of plants and algae. The organic matter in sewage acts as food for bacteria and as they use it they withdraw all the oxygen from the water thereby killing the fish. This is called eutrophication, or "over-enrichment". Industrial wastes may even contain chemicals and contaminants such as heavy metals which can only be removed by special treatments at the sewage processing plant.

THE GREAT LAKES

Domestic and industrial wastes discharged into the Great Lakes during the 1960s started to cause eutrophication. Sewage treatment has reduced this effect but there is still pollution from fertilizers, and problems with the build up of toxic chemicals.

Industry
Chlorides
Sulphates
Phosphates
Nitrates

COMBINED SEWERS

Drainage systems in towns have to handle the normal sewage flows as well as surface water produced by rain. The problem with a combined system is that heavy rain can overload the system and wash sewage out of the pipes. Separate storm drains only carry surface water and are less likely to cause pollution.

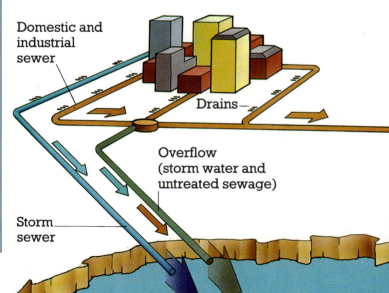

Domestic and industrial sewer

Drains

Overflow (storm water and untreated sewage)

Storm sewer

THE EFFECTS

Sewage discharged into the sea pollutes the water and beaches. Although the sight and smell of floating sewage is disgusting it is not that dangerous in itself. The main risk comes from infection by the unseen viruses and bacteria that travel along with the sewage and multiply in the favourable conditions.

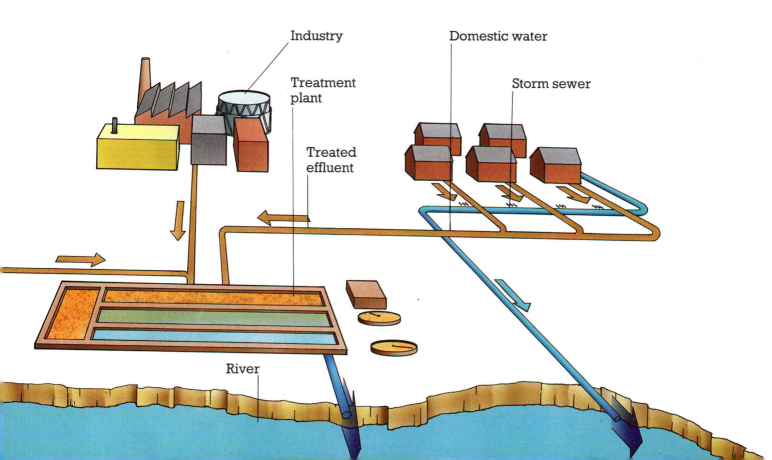

Industry

Treatment plant

Treated effluent

Domestic water

Storm sewer

River

WASHING MAKES WASTE

It is hard to think of crisp clean clothes as a source of pollution but they can be, indirectly. It is not the clothes themselves that are to blame, the problem lies in the detergents used to get them clean. Particular blame is attached to the phosphates that are used to prevent scum forming. They also act as a very effective fertilizer and pass through sewage works into rivers and lakes where they cause eutrophication. Foam is another problem people blame on detergents. Early detergents were particularly resistant to breakdown by bacteria and produced long-lasting foam that smothered rivers. Modern detergents break down more easily so foaming is much less likely to occur. Most are made from petrochemicals, but "green" detergents come from coconut oil.

MANUFACTURING SOAPS

Soaps are produced by treating fats and oils with caustic soda at high temperatures. Large quantities are still made by boiling in traditional open steel kettles that hold up to 1000kg at a time. The end result is a soft soap that contains about a third water. Perfumes and other additives are blended in and the soap is dried and processed to give bars or flakes. Most detergents are products produced by straightforward chemical reactions.

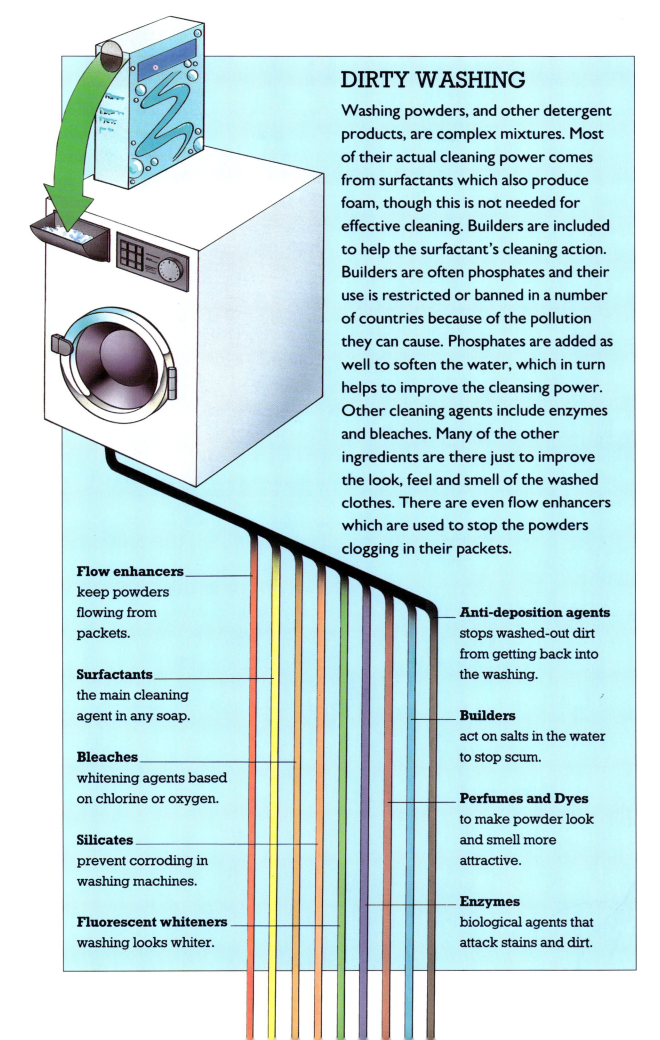

DIRTY WASHING

Washing powders, and other detergent products, are complex mixtures. Most of their actual cleaning power comes from surfactants which also produce foam, though this is not needed for effective cleaning. Builders are included to help the surfactant's cleaning action. Builders are often phosphates and their use is restricted or banned in a number of countries because of the pollution they can cause. Phosphates are added as well to soften the water, which in turn helps to improve the cleansing power. Other cleaning agents include enzymes and bleaches. Many of the other ingredients are there just to improve the look, feel and smell of the washed clothes. There are even flow enhancers which are used to stop the powders clogging in their packets.

Flow enhancers
keep powders flowing from packets.

Surfactants
the main cleaning agent in any soap.

Bleaches
whitening agents based on chlorine or oxygen.

Silicates
prevent corroding in washing machines.

Fluorescent whiteners
washing looks whiter.

Anti-deposition agents
stops washed-out dirt from getting back into the washing.

Builders
act on salts in the water to stop scum.

Perfumes and Dyes
to make powder look and smell more attractive.

Enzymes
biological agents that attack stains and dirt.

ALL IN THE AIR

Air pollution takes many forms, from smoke to photochemical smog and acid rain. Acid rain has been around for over a hundred years but the effects are cumulative. Today the problems it causes appear to be increasing rapidly. Fortunately the causes are known and solutions are available so we may be able to stop it getting still worse. Photochemical smog is produced when sunlight acts on a mixture of nitrogen oxides and hydrocarbons given off by car engines. Normally the products are dispersed into the atmosphere before smog can form but in some places the wastes are trapped close to the ground and smog can be produced. Limiting car exhaust emissions is the solution that has been adopted in some of the world's most developed countries.

EFFECTS ON NATURE

Acid rain is a continuing form of pollution that has long-term destructive effects. It is blamed for extensive forest damage and destruction and believed to reduce crop yields in the worst affected areas. Chemical changes caused by acid rain kill fish and other wildlife in rivers and lakes. Affected lakes are left clear and pure looking, but are actually devoid of fish and aquatic plants.

HOW IT HAPPENS

Coal contains small amounts of sulphur which is converted to sulphur dioxide when it is burnt. The gas is released into the atmosphere where it combines with water to form sulphuric acid and this falls back to the earth with rain.

Nitrogen from the air can also form oxides in high temperature flames. These oxides put nitric acid in the rain. The polluting gases can travel considerable distances in the atmosphere so acid rain often falls many miles from where the fuel was burnt.

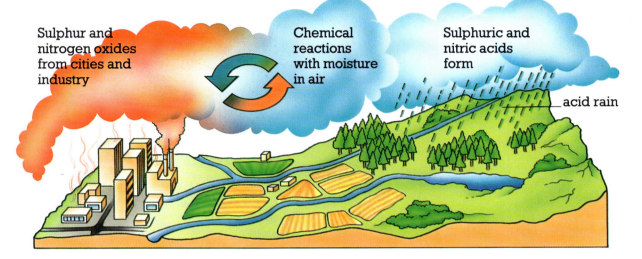

Sulphur and nitrogen oxides from cities and industry

Chemical reactions with moisture in air

Sulphuric and nitric acids form

acid rain

EFFECTS ON US

Acid rain eats into stone and concrete and is slowly destroying many important buildings and monuments. It corrodes unprotected metals and causes paints to peel. The direct health risks are small, although acid rain can affect particularly sensitive skins. Long-term risks appear more serious. Acid rain filtering down through the ground can dissolve poisonous heavy metals like copper and zinc. In time, the dissolved metals may find their way into the drinking water supplies and so into our bodies. Photochemical smog is a more immediate danger to health as it causes breathing problems and can put a strain on the heart.

DOWN IN THE DUMPS

Landfill dumps are the main way we get rid of industrial and domestic rubbish. However, the sheer volume of rubbish produced means that most of the suitable sites near towns have been filled up. Although everyone wants to have their rubbish taken away no-one wants to live next to a rubbish dump and it is getting harder and harder to find new tip sites. Properly planned and operated dumps are generally safe but serious problems can arise. As the waste decomposes it produces methane and this gas has to be got rid of before it can build up and cause an explosion. Landfill methane is therefore now being used as a fuel. Another serious problem is that rainwater trickling through the rubbish can produce a leachate that seeps from the bottom of the tip and pollutes the surrounding ground and waterways.

GETTING IT THERE

Refuse collection trucks can drive directly to tips that are near to town but in some cases the tips are more than 100km away. In these cases the rubbish is normally collected at a central depot and transported in bulk by train. One of the main problems with transporting rubbish is the amount that spills and pollutes along the way.

CLEANING OUT

When a tanker has delivered its oil some of the empty tanks are filled with water to act as ballast. The tanks also have to be cleaned out before they are refilled. These operations produce a sticky mixture of oil and water that has to be disposed of. Separators make it possible for the water to be discharged while controlling the discharge of this waste. The remainder is supposed to be stored on the ship for discharge at the port facilities, but dumping at sea still occurs.

INFILL DUMPS

In modern dumps the rubbish is piled in strips around 2m high and then covered with a layer of earth to stop it blowing about and to control smells. Successive layers are built on top of one another until the tip is full. A thick top layer of soil is then added. Methane produced by decomposition can be piped away for use as a fuel. Drainage systems cope with the leachate.

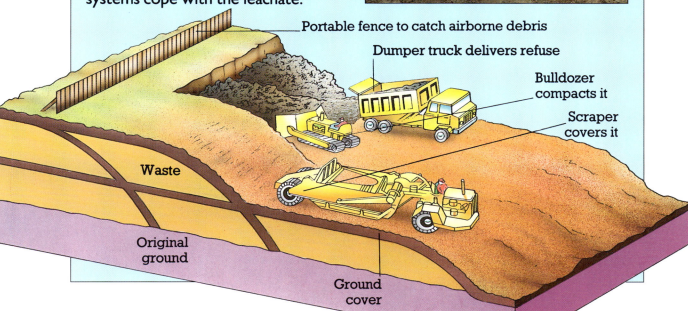

Portable fence to catch airborne debris

Dumper truck delivers refuse

Bulldozer compacts it

Scraper covers it

Waste

Original ground

Ground cover

BURNING QUESTIONS

Finding safe ways to get rid of toxic wastes is a real challenge. One of the best solutions is to burn them at high temperatures so the chemicals are broken down into their simplest constituents. Special equipment is needed to do this, trying to burn toxic chemicals in normal incinerators only partly breaks them down. It can even increase the risks by forming new compounds. Incineration is also being used to dispose of domestic wastes. The ash left after burning takes up a lot less space than the original rubbish and is easier to get rid of. Heat produced by the combustion process can be recovered and used for local heating schemes, or to even generate power. However, unless the furnace temperature is very high, toxic gases can escape. There have been a number of cases where people and pets living nearby have suffered from mysterious illness.

FINDING FACILITIES

There are only a few incineration plants that can handle toxic wastes properly and most operators want to know all about the waste before they will process it. This makes it very hard to get rid of mixed wastes, some shipments have spent months at sea trying to find somewhere to unload. Local and national protests stop disposal companies accepting particular waste consignments.

INCINERATORS

Incinerators operate at temperatures of up to 1200°C. A good supply of oxygen is provided and the toxic waste is kept in the combustion chamber until it is completely burnt. Gases produced by the incineration process are thoroughly cleaned before they are released. A high temperature incinerator can have a waste destruction efficiency of 99.9999 per cent for some of the most dangerous compounds. It can be 100 per cent efficient for others.

BY-PRODUCTS

Recovering pollutants can make good economic sense. Power station flue gases are cleaned up by using limestone slurry to wash the sulphur dioxide out. Calcium sulphite is produced and further processing converts this to the industrial raw material gypsum. Other flue gas treatments produce sulphuric acid or sulphur, both of which can be used by the chemical industry later on.

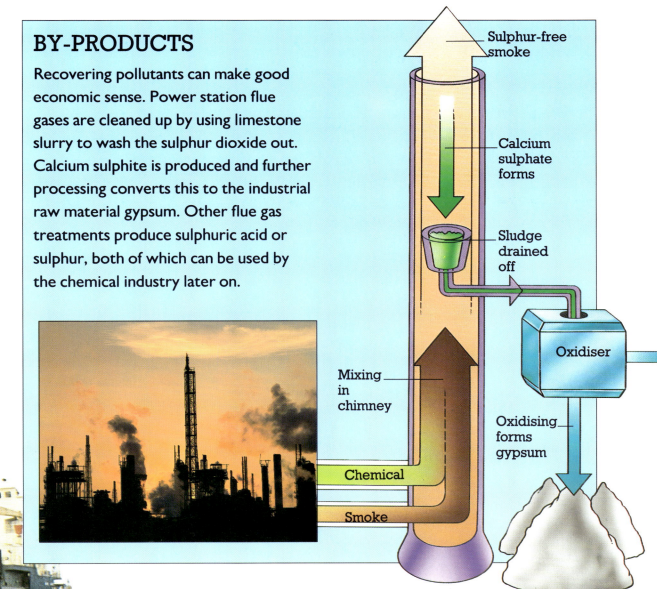

Sulphur-free smoke

Calcium sulphate forms

Sludge drained off

Oxidiser

Mixing in chimney

Oxidising forms gypsum

Chemical

Smoke

USEFUL RUBBISH

Most of the waste we throw away could be collected together and sorted into valuable sources of raw materials. As well as saving these materials recycling conserves energy and reduces the amount of rubbish that we have to burn or dump. The salvaged materials do not have to be particularly valuable to start with, most of them are so-called "disposable" items. Provided sufficiently large amounts can be collected on a regular basis it makes good economic sense to recycle low-cost products like aluminium, paper and glass. The best results are obtained by sorting the rubbish before it is thrown away since this keeps the costs of recycling low. Special collection centres like bottle banks and paper dumps encourage people to do this. In the long-term the advantages of recycling will be far reaching. It is predicted that it could cut down existing pollution problems by half.

SEPARATING IT

Modern processing plants separate mixed rubbish to recover the useful materials. Air classifiers blow a stream of air through the rubbish so light materials like paper and plastics are floated away for collection. Heavier rubbish is also separated by allowing it to fall through an air jet. The heaviest items, such as glass, fall straight through to a collection bin while less dense materials are deflected sideways into other bins. Iron and steel are collected with magnetic separators.

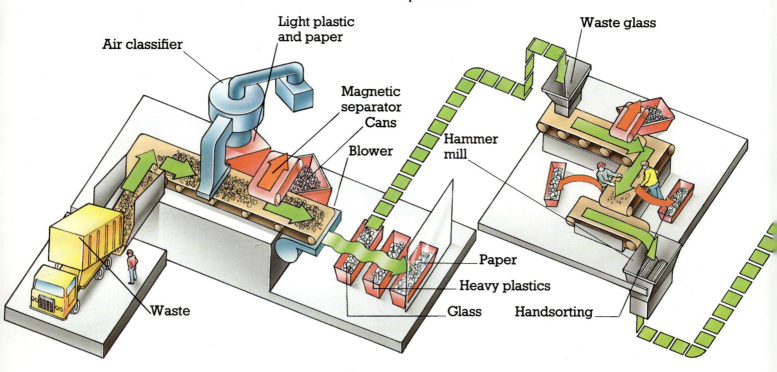

Air classifier

Light plastic and paper

Magnetic separator

Cans

Blower

Waste

Waste glass

Hammer mill

Paper

Heavy plastics

Glass

Handsorting

GLASS

Scrap glass collected in bottle banks and separated from rubbish is returned to the glass factories. After sorting into different colours the glass is broken up to make cullet which is one of the raw materials used for making new glass. In some countries more than half of the materials used for glassmaking are obtained by recycling.

PAPER

Reprocessing of waste paper produces a clean pulp for making new paper or cardboard. The paper is broken up and mixed with water to give a pulp which is treated to remove unwanted materials like dirt, staples and the glue used to hold magazines together. Washing and bleaching gets rid of the ink and leaves the pulp relatively clean. Reprocessing weakens the paper fibres so fresh pulp is also included in the mix.

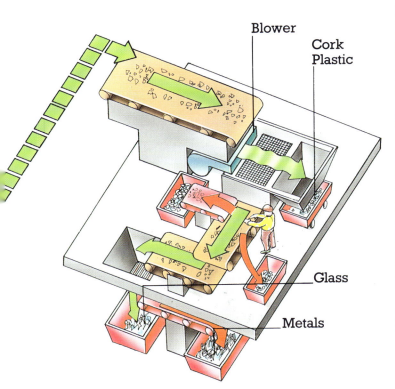

Blower

Cork
Plastic

Glass

Metals

METALS

Metals have always been recycled and scrap processing is a major industry. Metal objects that are no longer useful – from worn out cars and factory equipment to old bridges – are broken up and separated so the different materials can be recovered. Smaller items thrown away in the rubbish are also collected. The bulk of the material processed is iron and steel – scrap makes up around half of the metal used for steel production – but nearly all metals are recovered. High prices make it worthwhile collecting even small amounts of precious metals. Outdated electronic equipment is broken up for the gold-plating or copper on connections, and photographic chemicals are treated to recover the silver dissolved in them. Recycling metals also means a great saving in energy.

ALUMINIUM

Reprocessing scrap aluminium uses less than a tenth of the energy it takes to refine fresh metal from ore. Aluminium drink cans, for instance, are well worth collecting for recycling. It takes 31 barrels of oil to make one tonne of alluminium from imported bauxite ore. It only takes two barrels of oil when collected scrap is used instead.

THINGS TO KEEP

The variety of materials used in modern products, and the way they are combined, can make recycling difficult. Traces of other metals in steel scrap may make the new steel brittle and difficult to form. Advanced scrap preparation and refining methods can give effective separation of individual materials, but they also cost more. One solution is to design products which can be easily recycled.

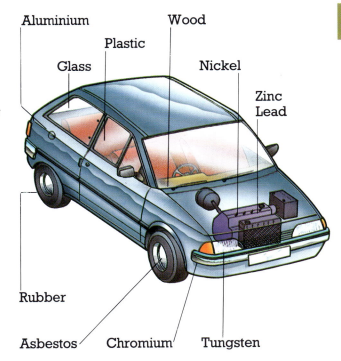

Aluminium
Plastic
Glass
Wood
Nickel
Zinc
Lead
Rubber
Asbestos
Chromium
Tungsten

SAVINGS

Modern mini-steelmills rely on a steady supply of steel scrap as their raw material. The scrap is loaded into electric arc furnaces and rapidly melted down ready for casting. In contrast, producing steel from ore involves smelting the iron oxides with coke in a blast furnace to produce liquid iron. This is then transferred to a second furnace where it is refined to make the steel.

ORGANIC AND PLASTIC

Organic materials like food scraps and vegetable waste are fairly easy to get rid of. In landfill they will normally rot down quickly. Used in a garden compost heap they can be converted into manure within a year. The same fermentation process is used to turn waste and sewage into compost. Plastic waste is an increasing problem since it is very hard to get rid of. Most plastics will not rot away if they are buried, and burning them can release dangerous products into the atmosphere. Recycling them is not easy either, even though plastics can be readily sorted out from other rubbish. The trouble is that there are many different types of plastic. They get mixed up and sorting them into useful piles is a very time-consuming job.

PLASTICS THAT ROT

One way of dealing with plastic waste is to modify the plastics so they will break down more rapidly. This can be done by making them sensitive to the ultraviolet in sunlight, or by including materials that are attacked by ground bacteria. Just making the plastics break down is relatively simple, the real problem is controlling the process so it happens at the right time – after the plastic has been thrown away.

USING DECAY

When there is a lack of oxygen organic materials are broken down by bacteria using a process of anaerobic digestion. This produces a by-product which is a mixture of carbon dioxide and methane that can be used as a fuel. Generators using anaerobic digestion convert sewage and other organic wastes into fertilizer while producing the gas.

WASTE FACTS

The 1952 Great Smog in London was estimated to cause 4000 deaths. Smoke from open coal fires and power stations was the main cause.

Over 400 million people have obtained water near their homes since the UN designated 1981-90 the Drinking Water and Sanitation Decade. But over 1000 million still have no easy access to safe drinking water.

Mercury waste discharged into the sea at Minamata during the 1950s caused severe nervous disease amongst villagers eating contaminated fish. There were 43 immediate deaths and many more victims suffered permanent disability.

Rain acidity is measured on the pH scale. The lower the reading the greater the acidity with a change of one unit representing a ten times increase acidity.

Pure water has a pH of 7, acid rain a pH below 5.6.

Love Canal, New York was used as a dump for more than 43,000 tonnes of chemical wastes during the 1940s and 1950s. Houses and a school were built on the site but the dump started leaking toxic chemicals. Some 240 families had to be evacuated. There are a lot of other chemical dumps in the same area.

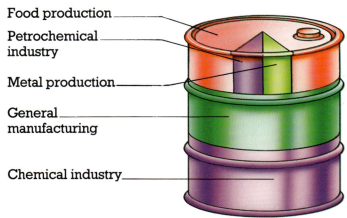

Food production
Petrochemical industry
Metal production
General manufacturing
Chemical industry

Severe pollution   Moderate   Occasional

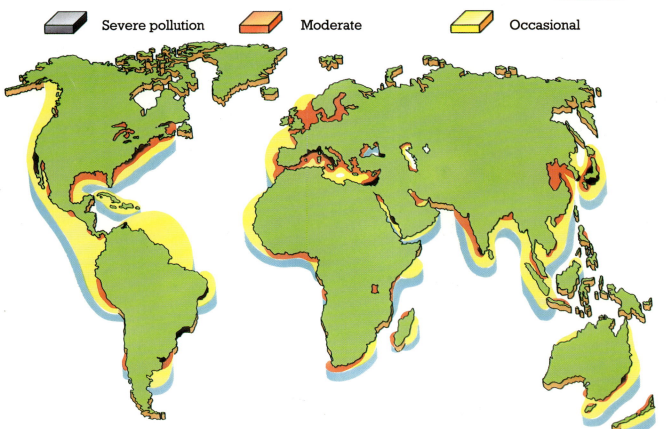

GLOSSARY

Bacteria single celled micro-organisms. Some types break down material by decay, others can carry disease.

Detergent synthetic cleaning agent used with water to wash dirt off or out of something.

Dioxins a group of highly poisonous chemicals, not deliberately manufactured but the by-products of certain chemical processes. Some occur when plastics are burnt.

Environment all of the factors which act on a living thing. It is often used to mean the surroundings we live in.

Eutrophication a process in which lakes, rivers or seas receive inputs of plant nutrients. If too much builds up within a body of water there is an excessive growth of algae which will use up all the oxygen and kill off the fish.

Landfill disposal of solid waste by tipping and covering with layers of earth.

Leachate liquid that has seeped through a waste tip and dissolved out toxic substances.

Organic to do with living things. Sewage liquid and semi-solid waste from houses, offices, farms and factories are all examples of organic material.

Toxic poisonous, liable to cause death if absorbed by the body.

USEFUL ADDRESSES

Centre for Environmental Education, University of Reading, London Road, Reading, Berkshire RG1 5AQ

Chemical Industries Association, King's Buildings, Smith Square, London SW1P 3JJ

Commission of the European Communities, 8 Storey's Gate, London SW1P 3AT

Department of the Environment, Public Enquiry Unit, 2 Marsham Street, London SW1 P3EB

Friends of the Earth, 26-28 Underwood Street, London N1 7JQ

Greenpeace, 30-31 Islington Green, London N1

Health and Safety Executive, Baynards House, 1 Chepstow Place, Westbourne Grove, London W2 4TF

National Society for Clean Air and Environmental Protection, 136 North Street, Brighton, East Sussex BN1 1RG
Oxfam, 274 Banbury Road, Oxford OX2 7DZ

Water Services Association, 1 Queen Anne's Gate, London SW1H 9BT

National Rivers Authority, 30-34 Albert Embankment, London SE1 7TL

INDEX

acid rain 18, 19, 30
air pollution 6, 7, 18, 19, 22, 30
anaerobic digestion 29
ash 22

bacteria 31
beaches 8, 13, 15
bleaches 17
bottle banks 24, 25
by-products 12, 23

cars 7, 18
chemicals 14, 23, 26
coal smoke 6, 7, 19, 30
convenience foods 11

detergents 16, 17, 31
dilution 8, 12
dioxins 12, 31
disease 8, 9, 15
domestic waste 10-12, 14, 20, 22
drinking water 9, 30
dumps 20, 21

emission control 7, 18
enzymes 17
eutrophication 14, 16, 31

fertilizers 8, 14, 16, 28, 29
foam 16, 17
food 10, 11, 28

incineration 10, 12, 22, 23, 28
industry 7, 12-14, 20

landfill sites 10, 11, 13, 20, 21, 28, 31
leachate 31

metals 14, 19, 26, 27
methane 8, 20, 21, 28, 29

oil 21
organic waste 28, 29, 31

packaging 10, 11
paper dumps 24, 25
phosphates 16, 17
photochemical smog 18, 19
plastic 28
poison 6, 9, 12, 13

recycling 24-28
rubbish 10, 11, 20, 24-26

sewage 6, 8, 9, 14, 15, 28, 29
sewage treatment 8, 10, 14
smoke 6, 7, 18, 30
soap 16
sorting rubbish 24, 25

tankers 21
toxic waste 12-14, 22, 23, 31

water pollution 8, 9, 14-16, 18, 20
wells 9